KINGFISHER
READERS

level
2

African
Savannah

Claire Llewellyn

KINGFISHEI

D0281111

KINGFISHER

First published 2015 by Kingfisher
an imprint of Macmillan Children's Books
a division of Macmillan Publishers Limited
20 New Wharf Road, London N1 9RR
Basingstoke and Oxford
Associated companies throughout the world
www.panmacmillan.com

Series editor: Polly Goodman
Literacy consultant: Hilary Horton

ISBN 978-0-7534-3794-0
Copyright © Macmillan Children's Books 2015

9 8 7 6 5 4 3 2 1

1TR/1014/WKT/UG/105MA

A CIP catalogue record for this book is available from the British Library.

Printed in China

Picture credits
The Publisher would like to thank the following for permission to reproduce their material.
Every care has been taken to trace copyright holders. However, if there have been unintentional
omissions or failure to trace copyright holders, we apologize and will, if informed, endeavour
to make corrections in any future edition.

Top = t; Bottom = b; Centre = c; Left = l; Right = r
Cover Shutterstock/Chantal de Bruijne; pages 4–5 Shutterstock/Oleg Znamenskiy; 6–7 FLPA/Bernd
Rohrschneider; 7t Shutterstock/Hedrus; 8 FLPA/Imagebroker, Rolf Schulten; 9 FLPA/Ariadne Van
Zandbergen; 10 FLPA/Bernd Rohrschneider; 11 FLPA/Frans Lanting; 12t naturepl.com/Ann & Steve Toon;
12–13 FLPA/Mitsuaki Iwago/Minden Pictures; 13t FLPA/Frans Lanting; 14 FLPA/Frans Lanting; 15 FLPA/
Frans Lanting; 16 FLPA/ Michel and Christine Denis-Huot/Biosphoto; 17t FLPA/Winfried Wisniewski;
17b Shutterstock/ajman; 18 Shutterstock/Francois Loubser; 19 FLPA/Mitsuaki Iwago/Minden Pictures;
20t FLPA/Ingo Arndt/Minden Pictures; 20b FLPA/Imagebroker; 21 FLPA/Gael Le Roch/Biosphoto; 22
Shutterstock/Francois Loubser; 23 Shutterstock/Mike Dexter; 24–25 FLPA/Shem Compion; 25t FLPA/Bernd
Rohrschneider; 26 Corbis/Martin Harvey; 27 Corbis/DLILLC; 28 FLPA/Richard Du Toit/Minden Pictures;
29t Shutterstock/Pierre-Yves BabelonPierre; 29b Corbis/ HO/Reuters; 30 naturepl.com/Suzi Eszterhas;
31t FLPA/Bernd Rohrschneider; 31b FLPA/Frans Lanting.

Contents

What is the savannah?

The grasslands of Africa are called the savannah. They are wide-open, grassy spaces that stretch as far as the eye can see.

The savannah is home to some amazing wildlife. There are elephants, rhinos, giraffes and lions, and large **herds** of antelope, zebra and wildebeest.

A grassy habitat

It is always warm on the savannah. Each year there are just two seasons: a wet season when there is rain, and a dry season when there is none.

Grasses grow well in this **habitat**.
It is too dry for most trees, but a few
are dotted here and there.

The plant-eaters

Antelope, zebras and many other animals feed on the different grasses. There is enough food to feed huge herds.

Giraffes feed on the leaves and fruits of trees. By stretching their long neck, giraffes can reach the softest leaves at the very top.

An elephant family

Elephants move around the savannah. Female elephants live together in small family groups.

Each group is led by one of the older elephants, who decides where to eat, drink and rest.

When one of the females has a baby calf, her sisters, aunts and cousins help to look after it.

The predators

Predators are animals that hunt and kill their food. Scorpions hunt mice and insects. Lions hunt zebra and other larger **prey**.

Lions hunt together in a group. They hide in the grass and keep close to their prey. Then they sprint forwards and try to catch it.

Life in the open

On the savannah there is nowhere to hide, so grazing animals are easy targets. They are safer in a herd. Thousands of them keep watch. If there is danger, they all run!

Hunters need speed to catch their prey. Cheetahs can run faster than any other animal.

The scavengers

Some animals avoid hunting by feeding on scraps that others leave behind. These animals are called scavengers. Jackals follow lions so they can scavenge their kills.

Vultures use their strong, hooked beak to tug at rotting **carcasses**. These birds are like rubbish collectors, cleaning up food that other animals have left behind.

Birds on the savannah

Many birds live on the savannah. Small weaver birds feed on insects and seeds. These birds build a ball-shaped nest using grasses they weave with their beak.

Ostriches are the biggest birds
in the world. They are too heavy
to fly, but their long, powerful
legs mean they can run faster
than gazelles.

Out of the sun

Many animals shelter from the sun. Termites build their nests inside giant mounds of soil. Inside, it is airy and cool.

termites

termite mound

Aardvarks dig deep burrows to rest in during the day. At night they hunt for termites. They break open the nests with their sharp claws and mop up the insects with their tongue.

The dry season

In the dry season, the grasslands are very hot. Rivers and waterholes dry up and the grasses die. Their seeds wait in the ground for rain.

But animals cannot wait. They must find food and water if they are to survive. Many of them set off on long journeys, called **migrations**.

The great migration

Every year, over a million wildebeest migrate around the savannah, looking for water to drink and patches of grass to eat. The animals face many dangers. They cross rivers where hungry crocodiles lurk.

Many months later, the wildebeest start their journey home. They arrive back as the rainy season begins and new grass starts to grow.

People of the savannah

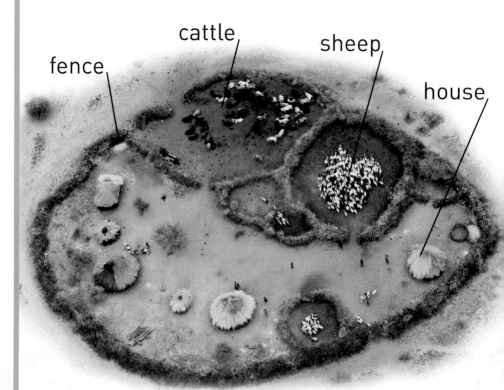

fence

cattle

sheep

house

People have always lived on the savannah. Once, they moved from place to place, but today they live in villages. Each village has a thick, thorny fence to keep out predators.

The people keep cattle, goats and sheep for their meat and milk. They sell the animals so they can buy things such as grain, school uniforms and beads.

Wildlife in danger

Today more people are farming the grasslands. This puts wildlife in danger. Some farmers shoot lions that attack their animals, or hippos that eat their crops.

Poaching is another danger.
Every year poachers kill thousands
of rhinos and elephants so they
can sell their horns and tusks. If the
killing doesn't stop, these animals
could become **extinct**.

Protecting wildlife

All across the savannah there are national parks, where animals are protected. Scientists and **rangers** track the animals and try to prevent poaching.

Tourists pay to visit the parks to
see the animals in their natural
habitat. This is
called going on
safari. Would you
like to go on safari?
Which animals
would you like
to see?

Glossary

carcass the body of a dead animal

extinct when an animal or plant has died out completely

habitat the kind of place where a plant or an animal lives

herd a group of animals of the same kind that live together

migration when animals move from one place to another for part of the year

poaching the hunting and killing of animals that are protected by law

predator an animal that hunts and kills other animals for food

prey an animal that is hunted by other animals

ranger a person who works to protect a natural place, such as a national park